Tough Topics

Divorce and Separation

Patricia J. Murphy

Heinemann Library
Chicago, Illinois

Photo research by Erica Martin
Designed by Richard Parker and Q2A Creative
Printed and bound in China by South China Printing Company

09 08
10 9 8 7 6 5 4 3

Library of Congress Cataloging-in-Publication Data
Murphy, Patricia J., 1963-
  Divorce and separation / Patricia J Murphy.
  p. cm. -- (Tough topics)
  Includes index.
  ISBN 978-1-4034-9775-8 (hardback) -- ISBN 978-1-4034-9780-2 (pbk.)
  1. Children of divorced parents--Juvenile literature. 2. Divorce--Juvenile literature. 3. Separation (Psychology)--Juvenile literature. 4. Broken homes--Juvenile literature. I. Title.
  HQ777.5.M85 2007
  306.89--dc22
                        2007005347

Acknowledgments
The publishers would like to thank the following for permission to reproduce photographs:
© Alamy pp. **12** (Mark Baigent), **14** (Steve Skjold); © Corbis pp. **6** (Simon Marcus), **8** (Zefa/Louis Moses), **10**, **11** (Image Source), **15** (Donna Day), **20** (Michael Prince), **24** (ROB & SAS), **25** (Zefa/Tim Garcha), **27** (Zefa/Charles Gullung); © Getty Images pp. **4** (Supershoot images), **7** (Jack Hollingsworth), **17** (Stone/Lonny Kalfus), **26** (Photodisc), **28** (Kris Timken Photography), **29** (Andre Gallant); © Jupiter Images p. **5** (Nonstock); © Masterfile pp. **9**, **23** (Jerzyworks), **13** (Rolf Bruderer); © Photolibrary pp. **16** (Bananastock), **18** (Photoalto), **19** (Stockbyte), **21** (Blend Images Llc); © Photolibrary.Com p. **22** (Australia)

Cover photograph of child with teddy bear reproduced with permission of © Corbis (Creasource).

Every effort has been made to contact copyright holders of any material reproduced in this book. Any omissions will be rectified in subsequent printings if notice is given to the publisher.

Contents

Some words are shown in bold, **like this**. You can find out what they mean by looking in the Glossary.

Separation and Divorce

▲ It is hard for parents to decide to separate or divorce.

When parents decide they want to live apart, they may separate or get a **divorce**. They may no longer get along, love each other, or want to be together anymore.

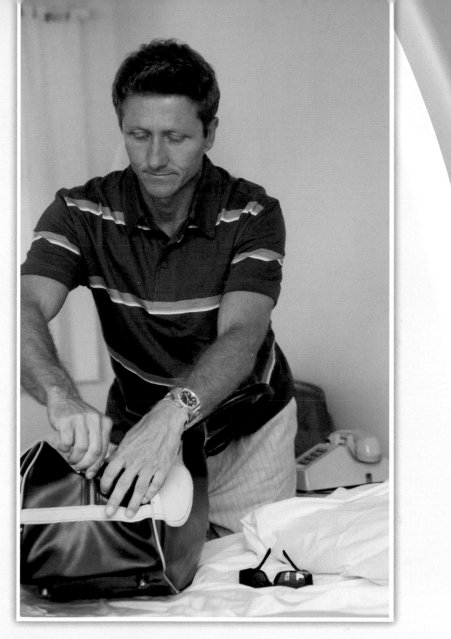

Separation or divorce will mean splitting up the family and other difficult changes. However, some parents decide that it is the best thing for their family.

Separation

A **separation** happens when two people decide that they want to live apart. They may be married or have lived together for a long time. A separation may last months or years, or it can be forever.

▶Moving out is a hard decision to make.

Most married people who get **divorced** separate first. They might use the time apart to think about what step to take next. Many of these couples eventually get divorced. A few may separate but then decide to get back together.

Getting a Divorce

A **divorce** is the end of a **marriage**. It is a **legal** agreement between two people who used to be married. A couple that wants a divorce hires **lawyers** to draw up divorce papers.

▲ Each partner signs the divorce papers.

▲ Divorce papers show that two people are no longer married to each other.

The divorce papers explain which parent the children will live with, and how often the children will see the other parent. After several months, the divorce is final. It is now law.

Living Apart

Usually when parents separate or **divorce**, children live with one parent. In some families, children might live with each parent part of the time. Some children may have to move to a new town and change schools.

When children are with one parent, they can keep in touch with the other parent through phone calls, letters, email, or visits. Living away from either parent can be tough when families are used to seeing each other every day.

◄ Many children still want to have fun with both their parents.

Is It My Fault?

If your parents separate or **divorce**, you may feel **guilty** or think you are to blame in some way. You might believe that you did something that caused them to break up. This is never true.

▲ Some children may spend lots of time worrying about why their parents broke up.

▶ It is always better to talk about your feelings.

Talking about these feelings with your parents may help you understand that the break-up has nothing to do with you. It might also help you see that there is nothing you can do or say to stop it from happening. It is between your mother and father.

Do My Parents Still Love Me?

Because your parents may no longer love each other, you may worry that they do not still love you. You may also think that your parents would stay together if they really loved you.

▲ Talk to both of your parents about how you feel.

These worries, thoughts, and fears are normal. Remind yourself that your parents are **divorcing** each other, not you. A parent's love for a child is different. It never changes or ends.

How Does It Feel When Your Parents Break Up?

Like all children going through their parents' **separation** or **divorce**, you may experience many different feelings. You may feel scared when you first learn that they are splitting up. You might be afraid of what will happen to you and worry about your future.

◄ Sharing your feelings and getting answers may help ease your worries and fears.

It is important that you share your feelings with someone who will listen. You should also ask questions about the separation or divorce so you know what to expect.

Feeling Sad or Angry

It is natural to feel sad when your parents **separate** or **divorce**. You may feel sad that your parents are not together anymore and that one parent has to move out.

◄ You may feel especially sad when you think about the way things used to be.

▶It is important that you do not hurt yourself or others when you feel angry.

You may feel angry, too. When you feel angry, you might say or do things that you do not mean. Find a positive way to express your sadness or anger. Go ahead and cry, do an art project, or kick a soccer ball around. You may be surprised how much better you will feel.

19

Feeling Alone

When your parents are **separating** or **divorcing**, you may feel lonely at times. You may miss spending time together as a family and seeing the parent who has moved out. You might also spend more time with a grandparent or a babysitter.

◄ Sometimes, you may have to find things to do by yourself.

When you feel lonely, call or write your parent who has moved out or do something that you enjoy. You might also help around the house so the parent you live with has more free time to spend with you. If these things do not work or you start to feel worse, turn to someone for help.

Getting Help

▲ It might help to talk to your friends about how you feel.

Going through a **separation** or **divorce** can cause many different feelings. One day you may feel happy. Another day you may feel sad. However you may feel, it is important to share your feelings.

Talk to someone you trust and who listens well. Talk to one of your parents or another family member. If you do not feel comfortable talking to relatives or friends, you could try to talk to a teacher, or a **counselor**. These people may be able to help you.

▲ It might help to talk to a teacher or counselor.

Accepting Change

After some time has passed, dealing with your parents' **separation** or **divorce** will be easier. You will get used to the new changes and begin to accept them.

▲ You can still enjoy spending time with both your parents.

You may still secretly hope that your parents will get back together someday. Unfortunately, hoping will not make it happen. Most parents who separate or divorce will not get back together. However, they will still be a part of your life.

New Families

Once two people **divorce**, they are free to date and marry other people. Sometimes they remarry someone with children of their own. They may also choose to have children with a new partner.

Getting used to new family members will take time. After a while, you may grow to love your parents' new partners and children. Even though your parents may choose to love other partners and children, they will not love you any less.

New Beginnings

While your parents' **divorce** is the end of something, it is also a new beginning. You and your parents will discover new ways to live and be happy.

One day, you may realize that your parents' decision to separate or divorce was the right thing for your family. While you no longer live together as a family, you still have a family.

Getting Through Your Parents' Separation or Divorce

- Remember: your parents are **divorcing** each other—not you. Keep repeating this over and over again if you forget it.

- Keep your things at both of your parents' houses. This way you will feel at home at either house.

- Don't be afraid to tell your friends about your parents' **separation** or divorce. Friends are for good times—and tough ones, too.

- If you are having a hard time in school or getting into trouble, ask for help. A separation or divorce is not an easy thing for anyone to go through. Everything in your life might seem a whole lot harder while you are going through it.

- Remember: no two families are the same. Your family may be different now—but it is still your family.

Glossary

counselor person trained to listen and give advice

divorce legal ending to a marriage

guilty feeling bad for having done something wrong

lawyer person who has studied law and can give legal advice, and represent people in court

legal having to do with the law

marriage state or act of being married

separation when two people in a relationship decide to spend time away from each other

More Books to Read

Bingham, Jane. *Why Do Families Break Up?* Chicago: Raintree, 2005.

Cadier, Florence. *My Parents Are Getting Divorced: How to Keep It Together When Your Mom and Dad Are Splitting Up*. New York: Amulet Books, 2004.

Levins, Sandra. *Was it the Chocolate Pudding? A Story for Little Kids About Divorce*. Washington D.C.: Magination Press, 2005.

Weitzman, Elizabeth. *Let's Talk About: Divorce*. New York: Powerkids Press, 1996.

Winchester, Kent. *What in the World Do You Do When Your Parents Divorce? A Survival Guide for Kids*. Minneapolis: Free Spirit Publishing, 2001.

Index